THE TIP OF MY TONGUE

POETRY

A Scottish Assembly
Sharawaggi (with W. N. Herbert)
Talkies
Masculinity
Penguin Modern Poets 9 (with John Burnside and Kathleen Jamie)
Spirit Machines

ANTHOLOGIES

ed., *Other Tongues*
ed., with Simon Armitage, *The Penguin Book of Poetry from Britain and Ireland since 1945*
ed., with Mick Imlah, *The New Penguin Book of Scottish Verse*
ed., with Meg Bateman and James McGonigal, *Scottish Religious Poetry*

CRITICISM

The Savage and the City in the Work of T. S. Eliot
Devolving English Literature
Identifying Poets: Self and Territory in Twentieth-Century Poetry
Literature in Twentieth-Century Scotland
The Modern Poet
ed., with Henry Hart, David Kinloch and Richard Price, *Talking Verse: Interviews with Poets*
ed., *Robert Burns and Cultural Authority*
ed., *Launch-site for English Studies*
ed., *The Scottish Invention of English Literature*
ed., *Heaven-Taught Fergusson*

THE TIP OF MY TONGUE

Robert Crawford

CAPE POETRY

Published by Jonathan Cape 2003

2 4 6 8 10 9 7 5 3 1

First published in Great Britain in 2003 by
Jonathan Cape
Random House, 20 Vauxhall Bridge Road,
London SW1V 2SA

Random House Australia (Pty) Limited
20 Alfred Street, Milsons Point, Sydney,
New South Wales 2061, Australia

Random House New Zealand Limited
18 Poland Road, Glenfield,
Auckland 10, New Zealand

Random House South Africa (Pty) Limited
Endulini, 5A Jubilee Road, Parktown 2193, South Africa

The Random House Group Limited Reg. No. 954009
www.randomhouse.co.uk

A CIP catalogue record for this book
is available from the British Library

ISBN 0224 069683

Papers used by Random House are natural,
recyclable products made from wood grown in sustainable forests;
the manufacturing processes conform to the environmental
regulations of the country of origin

Typeset by Palimpsest Book Production Limited, Polmont, Stirlingshire
Printed and bound in Great Britain by Biddles Ltd, Guildford and King's Lynn

for Alice, Lewis, and Blyth

with love

. . . not the theory of dreams, but the dreams themselves . . .

James Hogg

CONTENTS

Fiat Lux   1

Credo   2

The Tip of My Tongue   3

Conjugation   4

Ferrari   5

Arbuthnott   6

Pilgrim   7

St Andrews   8

A Moment of Your Time   9

Double Helix   10

Emily Carr   11

Cicadas   14

The Bad Shepherd   15

Developing Worlds   16

The Auld Enemy   17

Planetist   18

The Opening   19

Mons Meg   20

Acceptance Speech   21

A Scottish Poet   22

Birthplace   23

Glasgow   24

St Andrews   25

To Robert Baron   26

Blue Song   28

Ceud Mile Failte   30

A Good Address   31
Identity League   32
Air Quality   33
Workman   34
Micro   35
Bionote   36
From the Top   37
Windfarming   38
Tree Dance   39
The Order   40
Wege Durch Das Land   41
Scots and Off-Scots Words   42
Prayer of Allegiance   43
Aberdeen   44
The Music Cleaner   45
Dreamers   46
John Muir Variations   47
Uist   48
Croy. Ee. Gaw. Lonker. Pit.   49
The Mithraeum   51

ACKNOWLEDGEMENTS

I am grateful to the editors of the following magazines and newspapers where some of these poems have appeared: *Edinburgh Review*, *Herald*, *Literary Review* (USA), *London Review of Books*, *Poetry Review*, *Quadrant* (Australia), *The Republic of Letters* (USA), *Scotsman*, *Stand*, *Sunday Herald*.

'Credo' was commissioned by Fiona McLean for BBC Radio 4 and was distributed at the 1999 London Proms; 'Fiat Lux' was commissioned by Dave Batchelor for BBC Radio Scotland; 'Croy. Ee. Gaw. Lonker. Pit.' and 'The Mithraeum' were part of 'Shrines and Lights', a programme about Hadrian's Wall commissioned for the BBC Radio 4 series *Up against the Wall* by Tim Dee; 'The Opening' was commissioned by BBC Radio Scotland; 'Blue Song' and 'To Robert Baron' were made for *The New Penguin Book of Scottish Verse* which Mick Imlah and I edited in 2000, and which was commissioned by Tony Lacey and Anna South; 'Conjugation' was commissioned by Carol Ann Duffy for her anthology *Hand in Hand* (Picador, 2001); 'The Auld Enemy' was commissioned with support from the University of St Andrews Scottish Studies Institute and the Scottish Arts Council, was part of BBC Radio 3's *Heaven-Taught Fergusson* series produced by Dave Batchelor, and appeared in my edited book *Heaven-Taught Fergusson* (Tuckwell, 2003); 'Identity League' was commissioned by Laura Donnelly of The Comedy Unit for BBC Scotland's *Taxi for Cowan* television series.

I would like to thank Alice Crawford and Robin Robertson for helping to shape this book.

FIAT LUX

Let there be braziers, holophotal lenses,
Polished golden flags, champagne and candles,

Let rays shine through the rose window of Chartres,
Let there be cowslips, myriad splats of rain,

Trilobites, new parliaments, red neon,
Let there be twin-stone rings and mirrorglass

Skyscrapers, glinting jumbos, Rannoch lochans
In which huge skies can touch down in the sun.

Let there be Muckle Flugga's phallic pharos,
Bug-eyed, winking tree-frogs; let there be

Grand Canyons, fireflies, tapers, tapirs, matches
Good and bad, simply to fan the flames.

Let there be lasers, Fabergé crystal eggs,
Hens' squelchy yolks, birch-bark's thin,

Diaphanous scratchiness, let there be you,
Me, son and daughter, let the Rhine

Flow through Cologne and Basle, let there be
Victoria Falls, Great Zimbabwe, hornets' wings,

Angels, cardboard, zinc, the electric brae.
Let there be both stromatolites and cows,

Llamas and zebras, dromedaries, cats,
Bens, buns and banns, let there be all,

End all, every generation, so the whole
Unknown universe be recreated

Through retinal cone and iris and religion.
As has been said before, let there be light.

CREDO

As a candle-flame believes in the speed of light
I believe in you.

As the shoelace of glass believes in the full grown eel
I believe in you.

As Perth in Australia believes in Perth in Scotland,
As an old hand's vein believes in a baby's wrist,

Since what we cannot speak about we must,
As worlds have done, still do, will do, I make

For you, to you, in you, now and through this
My declaration of dependence.

THE TIP OF MY TONGUE

Some days I find, then throw my voice
Deep down the larynx of Glen Esk,

Ears cocked to catch what rumbles back,
English-Scots-Gaelic hailstones.

Other days the tip of my tongue
Is further off than Ayers Rock.

I'm lost for words, or find inside them
A pentecost that isn't tuned in.

I dream I'm a Shetland winterlight
Shining where you drowse in your nightdress,

Dreaming too, your book beside you,
In your hair an aigrette of ferns and beads of rain.

Enough said. Or of waking at a lover's angle
With you on the tip of my tongue.

CONJUGATION

I love the bigamy of it, the fling
Of marriage on top of marriage.
Marry me, Alice, marry my secrets,
Sight unseen, and marry Glasgow and Rose
Macaulay and the snell east wind.
I'll marry you and Iona and has-been,
Shall-be firths of slipways and dwammy kyles.
I do, you did, we'll do, hitched to every last
Drop of our wedding-day showers,
Downpours, reflecting us over and over,
So we'll fall in compact mirrors, blebs
As the heavens open, bride's veil, grey suit, ringing
Wet with carillons of rain.
That day seems like only tomorrow,
Present, future, pluperfect, perfect smirr
Champagning us doon the watter, on,
Launching us, conjugating each haugh,
Oxter, pinkie and lobeless lug
As it will be in the beginning.

FERRARI

Student poser, Presbyterian swami,
When Being and Nothingness ruled the Kelvin Way,

I rebelled by carrying a rolled umbrella
To lectures. I never finished *La Nausée*.

Chaperoned through suburbs by my virginity,
My act of Existential Choice was pie,

Beans and chips at Glasgow's boil-in-the-bag
Student Ref. Couscous? I'd rather have died.

Nightlife was homelife, the tick-tock soothe
Of a bowling club clock, long darning needles' hint

Of suture, so homely and sharp;
Each birthday, a wrapped after-dinner mint.

So, years later, graduated to the glassy Minch,
On the Castlebay ferry, leaning over its rail

Where, below us, a harnessed sailor
Sang from a cradle, painting the ship as it sailed,

I knew, stroking your breasts beneath your blouse,
Both being and nothingness. We kissed like a cashless king

And queen who've just splashed out and bought
A Ferrari for the first day of spring.

ARBUTHNOTT

Gales churn cornfields to a golden stushie,
North Sea haar dooks the North Sea.

Later, from Kinneff round past Dunnottar,
Heat vectors everywhere. Sunned kirks surmount

Peninsulas of cloud, wisps of the land.
Sound is a Triumph Herald, crickets. South,

Brechin Round Tower soars, a slim
Minaret of the Mearns.

On the swings, one minute
Feet on the ground, the next all up in the air,

I catch how Kincardineshire sky's
Transvaalish, Budapesty, Santa Barbaran,

Zurich on a perfect day. I love the North East
Everywhere of it, how it just zeros

On and on, then flauchters back
So zircon, so azure, so Alice blue.

PILGRIM

for Alice

Lighter than a snailshell from a thrush's anvil,
Glimpsed in grass cuttings, whiffs of splintered light,

But knee-tough, toddler-fierce and undeflected,
Slogging between Arbirlot and Balmirmer

Where the Arbroath road shoogles in the heat,
All plainchant and sticky willie,

E-babble and cushie doos,
A soul, like the signal from a mobile phone,

Heads south where muscadine light
Slurs mile-long midsummer breakers,

And sings out, blithe, by a kirk whose bellrope
Hangs, a frayed leash that's attached to the whole of the sky.

ST ANDREWS

I love how it comes right out of the blue
North Sea edge, sunstruck with oystercatchers.
A bullseye centred at the outer reaches,
A haar of kirks, one inch in front of beyond.

A MOMENT OF YOUR TIME

for Kate Whiteford

Z-rods and a Pictish hoopla of carved rings
Swim into view. Yachtsails on the North Sea
Tack back and forth, xeroxing other summers
When other yachtsails did that too, sped, idled,
Veered into light. Dwamtime. Heat-haze. Relaxed,
Unchronological ribbed fields. Leylines
Flounce across territories never ours,
Where we belong. Grassed-over souterrains
Rich with mud-rhythms, moss-haired residues
Of moon and beaver, lily, loon and quine,
I praise you all. Wind-sough, wind-sook
Of chamber-music, cairn-singing, firths'
Haar threaded through a net, babbling with dew,
Murmur me, let me catch another's breath,
Lightly, as part of breathing. Here it is:
Remnant, keepsake, rune, God-given script
Made just for you, the right lines, sacred text
Of matter cooked in stars, instantly endless,
Then passing on but holding nothing back,
Good for the child, the skeletal, the green
Foliage-bank whose sap's stared into at
Eye level. Here's the whole shebang that is
Time, place and climate, ebbing, dancing, set
In stone and motion, calmly at the ready
Before and after, purled in helices,
Every last atom pregnant with an A.

DOUBLE HELIX

Lemon after lemon, men harvest the drinkable light
Of California. Drilled into, aquifers open
To the heat, rising and falling, new geysers
Spring by a freeway whose cars, in pheromone lines,
Head north or south. Some stop to take stock, the surprise
Of lemonade in their hands. Licking her pinkie,
One driver watches columns of water. Stars
Come out of nowhere, like steps in the Okanagan,
An Okanagan of the night sky, where steps
Are light years between stars, where columns of water
Are rarer than an extra pinkie on human hands.
A comet passes. Its surprise stops trucks, to take stock
Of the pheromone trace of light above rows of cars
Parked in the night's heat. Rising and falling,
Open to our air, floodlit fountains from aquifers
Jet up wet light that might taste of lemon after lemon.

EMILY CARR

for Alice and Marjorie

Klee Wyck   Laughing One   they call
Through soaked air   on Vancouver   Island
Where she snores   adenoidally   in roadmakers' toolsheds
Inches down   night-chilled   slimy rungs
To the   tippiness   of a canoe
One   woman   British Columbia
Nosing   among floating   nobs of kelp
The bay   buttered over   with calm

Parents   christened her   Emily Carr
Wee faces   scribbled   on her fingernails
Black curly hair   chipmunks   white rats
Zigzagging   through Beacon   Hill Park
Tiptops   of redwoods   eightsome reeling
Stravaiging   to classes   out in San Francisco
Charcoaling   a big   plaster foot

Jazzily   in Paris   she misses the ocean
At Skidegate   and dank   Kitwancool
Among Fauves   underneath the Eiffel   Totem
Pines   for where colour   throbs out in the woods
Asthmatic   mutilated   enriched
She sits   a stilled   tongueless bell
Among   smallpoxed   poles in the forest
'No one   to shake hands with   but myself'
Eyeing   carved beaks   head-high nettles
Burst seams   of a cheap   Indian coffin
A logger's saw   purrs   on the beach
'Don't tether yourself   to a dishpan   woman'
Shorelines   mew   like a cat

Her perjink father   so worshipped   England
He lugged it here   locked   in a camphor-wood chest
Pulpy   prayerbooks   books of psalms
Jesus Christ   out in   Tanoo
Nailed to a pine   then risen   holes
In his hands   for the wind   to blow through

Up the Skeena   mosquitoes   filling her mouth
Totem poles   with mouthlike doors   in their bases
Letting you   breeze   in and out
She catches   a hoydenish   Knock Knock
Who's There   drummed   in each trunk
Deep   through its unpeeled   fungal bark
Treks on   finding   forsaken poles
Colourless   toneless   soaked in grey paint
Waterbarrels   scummy   with greenish slime
Jam kettles   rusted   in rain
Breathing   mosquitoes   head in a sack
With a hole   for a panel   of glass
Two pairs of gloves   canvas   pantalettes
Loose   to the soles   of her shoes
She sketches   obliterated   ravens
Inspired and   hurrying   against the clock
Everything   is made   out of breath

Needlingly   shining   in hundreds and thousands
The Godhead   at Skedans   is not
Stuffily   squeezed   in a church
More like   a string vest   a drystone wall
Looseknit   mortarless   blown not so much
Here in the cutaway   lower   branches
But the very   tips   of the pines

White housepaint   mixed   with artists' colours
Eked out   with canned   gasoline
PAINTINGS   mounted   on mosquito netting
Lying alone   out in   the caravan
Praying hard   devilfish like sausage   sweet
Life smells   coal-oil   turps
Soaps   powder   disinfectant
Rubber of   well worn   hot water bottle
Camp fire   birdsong and pine trees   one
Sweetness   in your head   and out it

Coughing   with eight bunched   shaggy dogs
Her creaky   big black   baby carriage
Weighed down   with beans   and her Javanese monkey
Chomping   a suburban   earwig
Where a parson   thwacked a cat   with a plank
Gulped   in the stomach   of that timbered room
Where all the totems   were telephone   poles
Out in   Victoria   near Parliament House
On buff ceilings   sea eagles'   outspread wings
Breathlessly   wanting   to carry her off
To try   the high air   of Okanagan

Wind's spank   a beaver's   silent scoot
Totem poles   splitting   in the island woods
North wind   out in   a hessian flour sack
Billowing it   as if   it were silk
Best   of all things   Emily Carr
Gave us   when she   was dead
High   in the treetops   hoaching with ravens
Yon green   Victorian   unVictorian
Throughing   and throughing   of the wind

CICADAS

from the Greek

Alcman

The tops of the bens and the benside burns are asleep
With nesses and steep-sided glens –
All the dark, Gaian larder,
Wildcats and heather-honey bees,
Fins and tails deep in porphyry sealochs –
And the songbirds are flying in their sleep.

Sappho

That cloud-juiced apple at a high twig's tip,
Reddening on the utmost branch.
The one the apple-pickers missed.
Not missed. They could never reach it.

Meleager

Though the garland round Heliodora's head
Fades now, she sparkles, she is herself
A garland to garland the garland.

THE BAD SHEPHERD

I am the bad shepherd, torching my flocks in the fields,
Feeding them accelerant, hecatombs of wedders and tups.
In pits or pyres all are sheared and shamed by the flames.
Every sheep is a black sheep in that fire,
Penned in by heat, conspicuously consumed.
If one escapes when ninety-nine are burned,
Hunt it down. Best now my lambs are lost
So sheep are shelved, or vaporised unsold,
Hanging in charred clouds – hairst hogs, maillies, and crocks.
Cloned palls cover Cumbria. Shadows slur Lockerbie's drumlins.
Cling, braxy, scrapie, tremmlin, pindling, all
Diseases of sheep go huddled together in one
Beltane burn. *Ca' the yowes to the knowes* . . .
I am the bad shepherd. Follow me.

DEVELOPING WORLDS

for Robin Robertson

Jungles, lemurs, snoods, and Asian tigers
With stone, bare-breasted girls at Nakhon Wat

Albumed in albumen. John Thomson – so
Saturated with collodion,

Pictures could be developed from his flesh –
Snaps couched Victorian debs with entrepôts'

Formosan raspberries, goldfish in vases,
Cool, floating temples captured after dawn.

Bearers with lead-lined packing cases take
Forbidden cities held in his emulsions'

Deliquescent, slewed, chemical time,
So Scotland sees by oxyhydrogen light

Khmer jungles flare through Sauchiehall Street rooms,
Hong Kong Scots pose, and spectral odalisques

Mix with Foochow beggars and cold Lambeth's
Poor souls, a hackit widow with a cup,

Street people from one empire or another,
Grinning, nursing, gambling, writing, sleeping,

Recruiting, peeping, dreaming, dressing, crying,
Each snatched glance worlds apart, each glance our own.

There they are, bonny fechters, rank on tattery rank,
Murderer-saints, missionaries, call-centre workers, Tattoos,
Bunneted tartans weaving together
Darkest hours, blazes of glory,
Led by a First Bawheid, rampant, hair fizzin, sheepsheared,
Scrummin doon, pally wi their out-of-town allies,
Wallace fae Califaustralia, Big Mac, an Apple Mac,
Back from the backwoods, wi Rob Fergusson, Hume, Sawney Bean –
See how yon lot yawn and yell and stretch
Right owre from Blantyre tae Blantyre, Malawi!
Wait till ye catch the whites o their eyes, aye,
The specky, pinky-flecky whites o their eyes
Worn out from ogling down a Royal Mile o microscopes, or fou
Wi dollars n yen signs, or glaikit wi bardic blindness. Wait
Till ye hear their 'Wha daur meddle wi me', their hoochs
And skirls of 'Rigour!' Wait till ye smell
Through coorse, dauntless, distilled Jock courage,
The wee, trickling smell of their underdog-on-the-make fear
Dribbling down greaves, rusting nicked, spancelled armour.
Wait till you hear the start of those whispers,
'We're fine, thanks, Tony.' 'Don't rock the boat.'
'Oh, thank you, thank you, Secretary of State.'
That's the time, eyeball-to-eyeball,
Tae face them down, the undefeated
Canny Auld Enemy, us.

PLANETIST

I love all windy, grand designs, all blashes
Splattering the dark, heaving the moon

High over spruces, under the weathered
Cloud rivers turning in their beds.

From the tip of my tongue to the pit of my stomach,
From my eyeballs to the balls of my heels

With my lanky body I thee worship,
Scotland, New Zealand, all national dots,

The salt of the earth, the pepper of the earth,
The oregano of the world –

But I'm a planetist as well,
Singing your praises, honoured speck,

Stung with sleepless inspiration
When even the wind has emphysema,

Roads, keep right on to the end of yourselves,
Islands, keep your heads above water.

THE OPENING

We have a crown no queen or king can wear.
Kings used to wear it, till they wore it out.

Drop it. Leave it behind on that long road
Forking to India, Canada, the Cape –

Past Guy Fawkes bonfires dowsed with Burns Suppers –
We took to reach this Scottish Parliament.

Watch champagne corks soar in eyes-up arcs
Heady as the whoop! whoop! whoop! of Beltane dancers

Leaping through the flames, faster and faster,
Sparks at their heels, away, hats in the air.

MONS MEG

for my daughter

Under warmed, antiseasonal skies
Zoo capercailzies flap away

Towards the terminus of species;
Headsetted tourists evolve into

Cyborgs on the Castle ramparts;
But I have ears and eyes only for you,

Wee ballerina, pas-de-bas-ing in front of Mons Meg,
Singing down the barrel of that gun.

I love how you yell a pirouette,
'Hullo, Mons Meg! Goodbye, Mons Meg!'

Blithe beside its heavy, pitch-black muzzle,
Laughing in the cannon's mouth.

ACCEPTANCE SPEECH

I want to thank each bead of water
In Lake Baikal and polar Lake Vostok.

Thanks, too, to that Zurich Zoo chimp for taking
Her vertical stroll up a rope,

And to stones – strong, geriatric gneiss
In the hip-deep soil of the world.

As a Scot, I know I owe a debt
To rain. That supportive, laundering drench,

From taiga forest to typhooned Macao,
From whitening Great Barrier Reef

To the drawdown of the Ogallala,
Has made our wandering, once-and-future

Ambassadors feel at home.
Danke schön, planet, for your gift of tongues,

More than I can ever say:
Norwegian, hydrangea, Aztec, Vietnamese.

I know things might have been better done
Had Thomas Midgeley never exhaled

Lungfuls of CFC;
But today belongs to the pink camelia,

Tormentil's medicinal, astringent roots,
Grouse feathers, kisses, websites,

Marquetry. Last of all, prayerful thanks
To that opal-blue inch snatched through the pines

Years overhead, which a raven crossed,
Gliding from sight beneath invisible

Transhumant stars, each reminiscent
Of everywhere in particular.

A SCOTTISH POET

At my cubbyholed desk I work outdoors
Through blash and sun in Skye and Lingo, Fife,

Yearning and earning, a fikey, deskbound shaman,
Trying to let the side up.

I love it, the mouth music's make and break
Between lines – earthed Callanish standing stone,

Dry and thin as Donald Dewar,
Or levitating Scott Monument, landed

On Edinburgh's lunar surface.
I work out, too, on each of those eastcoasty moons,

St Andrews, Carnoustie, Kirriemuir,
Satellites in the outback of Avizandum,

My job description just one long
Sabbatical from real life.

Always good, though, work after work,
Commuting to my second, third, and fifth homes

In Glasgow, Hoy, or smeeky Kirkcaldy,
Feet up on every computer in Scotland,

Floating into my anxious trance,
Vatically without honour,

Or, calmed, near Bishop Elphinstone's tomb,
Candle-lit in his lyrically squint chapel,

By voices singing of 'ingens Bennachius'
And Benachie's reddening apples.

BIRTHPLACE

translated from the Latin of Arthur Johnston (1587–1641)

Here, neck and neck with the Vale of Tempe,
Stretches the Howe of the Johnstons.
Underneath Aberdeenshire sky
The sparkling, silvery Urie Burn
Slaloms over well-fed farms.
Benachie's sgurr untousles a last quiff of cloud;
Night and day hang in the balance.
The Don hides garnets. The high glens, too,
Dazzle with gemstones, pure as India's best.
Nature reclines *au naturelle*
On a surging bed of heather. Swallows
Loop in the tangy air. Salmon
Flicker. Strong-bodied cattle
Chew the cud in the pastures.
Here, where northern apples redden,
Cornfields bend under golden grain,
Largesse lets orchards sag.
I sprang from this, these rivers, fields
Over a hundred generations
Always the Howe of the Johnstons.
Virgil made his birthplace famous;
Mine will be the making of my poems.

GLASGOW

translated from the Latin of Arthur Johnston (1587–1641)

Head held high among sister cities,
Glasgow, you are a star.
Gulf Stream winds defrost you. No fear, though,
Of your being frazzled to a crisp at high noon.
The Clyde sweeps through, detoxed like amber,
A thousand ships flying your flag.
Ashlar bridges you, bank to wet bank,
Granting all comers safe passage.
Round about, orchards and roses
Up the Clyde Valley, a Paestum of the distant west,
Woodnymphs, each lithe as a salmon.
Town centre tenements' flashbulb brilliance
Hides wall-to-wall Style; sheer marble
Churches to die for. Down the road
Rat-a-tat patter stuns the Sheriff Court.
Bang in the middle, your University
Sings hymns to Phoebus Apollo.
You make the gods grin, my favourite Glasgow.
Sea, earth and air have ganged up to make you shine.

ST ANDREWS

translated from the Latin of Arthur Johnston (1587–1641)

Sacred St Andrews, the whole wide world
Saw you as the burgh of God.
Jove, eyeing your great Cathedral,
Blushed for his own wee Tarpeian kirk.
The architect of the Ephesian temple,
Seeing yours, felt like a fake.
Culdee priests in holy cassocks
Gazed through your East Neuk of light.
St Andrews' Archbishop, clad in gold,
Bellowed at Scotland's Parliament.
Now that's gone, walls ankle-high,
Priestly *fiat lux* tarnished.
Still you pull poets, though. You wow
Lecturers and lab technicians.
Aurora of the Peep o' Day in Fife
Frisks ashore with salt-reddened fingers,
Herring-sparkle of dawn.
Thetis coughs through 10 a.m. haar,
Waking hirpling, hungover students
Who sober up with golfclubs.
Phocis was Phoebus's long-time lover,
Attica of Pallas. In St Andrews
Each dances. Forever. Now.

TO ROBERT BARON

translated from the Latin of Arthur Johnston (1587–1641)

Dear Doctor Baron, Aberdeen,
Read this, my mudstained, gloomy work
Sent from a burn that feeds the Don.
Out on my croft, far out of town,
Among rough, stony, worn-out fields,
Ex-poet, and ex-learned man,
I plough my furrow with dour beasts.
Bent double, eyes glued to the clods,
I trek behind my oxen's lines,
Goading them on or chanting verse,
Teaching the ox boustrophedon.

Sometimes I hoe and hoe the marl,
Sometimes I harrow it to death,
Or jab it. With my writing hand
I haul the stones from new-ploughed fields
Then, maybe, irrigate the land,
Or drain it with a shallow pit.
Both arms ache with threshing crops,
Both feet are just about done in.
Stripped off, I fork muck with a graip,
Then spread dung on the heavy soil.
Arcturus winks. I scythe my crops.

Some of the harvest's scorched, ground down,
Some of it's in the Gadie burn.
Through the hot summer I prepare
For snow, cutting and banking peat.
Excavating the earth's bowels
I just about see spooks and think
The dead peer back. What makes it worse,
As when a storm first hits and then
Wave after wave pounds in, my head's
Just touched the pillow in pitch dark
When I'm awoken by the lark.

My overalls are shaggy pelts.
Breakfast's a turnip once again,
The Gadie burn to wash it down.
I'm dying in a thousand ways –
The Underworld might cheer me up –
So lonely, scared the mirror shows
Not who I was. Teeth like a dog's,
Hair dandruff-white, boils on my lips,
I take my stand knee-deep in shite,
Bowed-down, too harnessed to the plough,
Downcast, the beast I have become.

BLUE SONG

(made by Mary, daughter of Red Alasdair, soon after she was left in Scarba)

after the Gaelic of Mary MacLeod (c.1615–1705)

Hoireann o

I am sad
since a week ago

left on this island,
no grass, no shelter.

If I could
I'd get back home,

making the journey
rightaway

to Ullinish
of white-hoofed cattle

where I grew up,
a little girl

breast-fed there
by soft-palmed women,

in the house of brown-haired Flora,
Lachlan's daughter,

milkmaid
among the cows

of Roderick Mor
MacLeod of the banners.

I have been happy
in his great house,

living it up
on the dancefloor,

fiddle-music
making me sleepy,

pibroch
my dawn chorus.

Hoireann o ho bhi o,
Ro hoireann o o hao o.

Say hullo for me
to Dunvegan.

CEUD MILE FAILTE

Iain Crichton Smith, 1928–1998

This morning I stare at frosty wavelets,
Expecting you to bob up,

Your silkie's head, hazel-bald and polished
In a spry wig of dulse, adrift between

Beijing and Garrabost, Yarmouth and South Australia,
Canada and Taynuilt, Paris and the village of Bayble,

Buoyed beside heroic tatters
Of Lewis or Harris, their gneiss and quartz

End-on to force elevens, sparkling.
Drowned learner choirs, sea-booted, garbling school hymns,

Haunt that white house through whose doorway you float,
Chatting with your friends in one room in English,

Calling to the others in Gaelic.
Your language lives with a tube down its gullet.

For every hundred thousand welcomes
An abrupt hundred thousand goodbyes.

A GOOD ADDRESS

Hair fizzing, earlobes red with daftness,
Hugh MacDiarmid in his council house

Or maybe out back, in its garden shed
A.k.a. The Scottish Poetry Book Club,

Retunes near planets till they mutter Doric
Sing-songily, but alien all the same,

Nane for thee a thochtie sparin',
Earth, thou bonnie broukit bairn! . . .

Up carpetless, dark-varnished, creaky stairs
Edward Baird's sables make 20s Montrose

El Greco's Toledo, shining over water,
A Scoto-Spanish, kirky Tir nan Og,

While Willa and Edwin Muir, in Willa's mum's
Draper's shop, talk sex, conscious that past

Their douce seaside cosmology of golfballs
Where fiddlers jig and 'The Democratic Butcher'

Places his doggerel in the local rag,
Immigrants flit – black swans, swifts, swallows, terns

To and from Africa, Siberia –
Native and foreign as the Pleiades,

The Royal Family, or a crystal set;
Birds' unpredicted, random, oiled quill-feathers,

Still frosted with aurora borealis,
Drop on the High Street's pavements, or Links Place.

IDENTITY LEAGUE

Duns Scotus   1   Harristotelian Ravers   1
Echt Weecaledonians   1   Scots Internationalists   1
Cock o' the South   1   Orkney Vagina Academicals   1
In Kirrie, where they sell hand-painted lightbulbs,
In St Andrews, where St Andrew never preached,
Through vennels, kennels, bennels, shrines and hoolies
From California Hall to Moscow, Ayrshire,
The needle match between Scotland and Scotland
Goes into extra time and never stops.

AIR QUALITY

for S. and G.

I forecast bright force-eights from the Bell Rock,
Hard, Trans-Siberian hail at Leuchars station,

Dum-Spiro-Spero, long, heartstopping puffs
Along the Scores, North Seas blue as the Med,

Yon never-never oxygen of Fife's
Blip microclimate. Draw that through your lungs

The way pipesmokers used to take Three Nuns,
Expensive breaths, in sickness and in health;

Breathe in frittered cathedral, golf carse, vennels
Chilled with an aftertang of burning flesh.

Inhale the distance, eyes on the horizon,
Exhale North Castle Street, inspired

On this tardis coast with all its airs and graces,
Radar, *Discovery*, the *Cutty Sark*.

Our Kingdom of the Anemometer.
Wherever you go, go like the wind.

WORKMAN

Stretched on his side in keen December sun
Along a ditch in his fluorescent jacket
Among thrawn grassblades, each a skelf of light,
Beside the road where Fife's old iron milestones
Are newly blank, the villages and farms
Indecipherably whited over,
Bleached Cairnhill, Feddinch, Wester Lathallan,
Lathockar Mains, Radernie and Lawhead,
Largoward, Baldinnie and Baldutho,
The roadman lies, breathily concentrating
Like a sniper or a mine-disposal expert,
Holding a fine brush primed with outdoor gloss
To last five years, slow letter by black letter
All afternoon repainting the names.

MICRO

Angström by angström, working
With resin, Willard Wigan
Sculpts only at night – less traffic, less vibration.
Inside a microscopic ring
Muhammad Ali fights Sonny Liston.
Wigan trains himself to slow down his heart
So he can work between beats.
Jab. The referee tilts towards the ropes.
The whole ring's smaller than a sulphur match-head.
One finger pulse could knock out the champ
Who would drown in a sweat-bead tsunami.
Vandals breathed away what many
Consider Wigan's finest work,
A tableau: Snow White and the Seven Dwarfs
Disneying in the eye of a needle.
Bottled flotillas pall beside splinters
Razored with dyslexic glee,
Housing schemes and slides for pet ants
Singled out from their species.
His website – theimpossibleworld.com –
A Birmingham invisible to the naked eye
Showcased for all to see,
Is all keyhole surgeons' handstand glances
Into the dry domain of the virtual
Before you wobble, log off, and silently
Tip back the right way up.

BIONOTE

Maybe related to racing cyclist, Fausto Coppi,
Though born in Dornoch, his dad 'a great
Catarrh factory of a man', mother a sanitary inspector;
'My childhood', he told Sartre, 'was filled with the sound of the pipes,
Interrupted by gouts, rheums, catexia,
Vertigo, wind, and too much codliver oil.'
Artschooled at Wick Plein Air College,
Our man chilled out with the Dunnet Head Group, then,
Stateside, slaved as Jackson Pollock's cleaner.
Slime obsessed him. Early works in salad cream and urine
Date from this time, though his father ate most of them
Immediately before his own death. Back home,
Sketching at a Fife badger-baiting, the artist
Lost his right arm, though he disliked the word 'lost',
Preferring to insist he knew exactly
Where it had gone. *Der Furzwerk*
Dates from that year, painfully fusing
Surrealism and constipation.
After he died from self-inflicted midgebites
In Wester Ross's only public toilet (which served
As his studio), word leaked out
Of one last, dark work, part lava, part lavvie,
Celebrating all his passion for Dornoch,
Entitled, 'Homage to Pan'.

FROM THE TOP

for Iain Galbraith

From the top, breathless, feet in the clouds,
I see how at the ankle-high horizon

Dutch fields are Berber rugs in a bazaar;
Red tiled roofs pave the village far below;

I clock the non-stop Colorado River,
Dandelion heads unblown in East Westphalia,

Bings, sunlit mesas of the Scottish Lowlands,
Stretching towards nettled woods whose watermills'

Dust harps, thick burr stones, and dark gavelocks
Promise half firlots or a grinding halt.

I spot South Island beckoning Amazonia
Past Arrochar and Wiesbaden, I watch

Shackleton's shadow cross the Southern Lights
And swallows brushing Arabic on air,

That canny man of 78 who built
The biggest sugar mills in Puerto Rico,

Horn spoons, a rotting, gnawed-at Hong Kong torso,
And Carrick Castle inlaid on Loch Goil,

All things improbable, as God's my witness,
Bamiyan Buddhas, Easter Island heads,

And everything I see here from the top
Is overlooked by bens and glens of stars.

WINDFARMING

Flailing outstretched cirrus fields,
Sleek metals throw up their hands,

Gleaning, milling where there is no corn
In the agribusiness of air,

Totempoled into acceleration's
Ultimate source and resource,

Propeller-driven crosses of the risen Christ,
Great ghosts of standing stones.

While everything is speeding up,
Overheating, hurtling away,

Good to stand still on this moonlit upland,
Canny, uncanny, with a choir of angels

Towering above us, beating their wings,
Piloting the earth on its way.

TREE DANCE

Dandering through Glen Convinth woods,
Fro and to, there and here,
I give up trying not to slip. A frog
Plops into hiding. Just about lost, I inch
Close to a pine and stare up its bark's
Arterial road to the clouds.
I lean against the dry, encrusted trunk,
My ear an inch from rings and resin, hiding,
Frog-quiet, out of the wind. All give,
There and here, to and fro
The tree sways, dandering in high blashes, rooted.
I sway with it, cheek to living cheek.
Each of us will last a lifetime.

THE ORDER

After a partnership that failed
Near dreich Port Glasgow, now at Yoker all

Went like a dream: the order
A sleek-hulled steam yacht for a German client

Due to be launched in late 1914.
That was the spring my mother's uncle sweated

And did not stop. He and his staggering wife
Went by unsteady train to Greenock West

To be looked after by my grandmother
Berthed in a tenement. Enteric fever.

He died, but the women lived through the Great War,
Which, though she was not thought of at Versailles,

Stopped just three years before my mother's birth;
And by the time her fluent Pitman's shorthand

Reached ninety words a minute, a bomb fell,
Blitzing the Greenock flat she had just left.

Next it's my turn, part of the post-War years,
Leverets scooting, fast as twanged elastic,

The shipyards closed, and, like an open book,
My young son can explain the human genome,

Letting me see in unassembled brass
Screws, handrails, greased pistons of an engine,

Bow-wave and wake, the stranded DNA
Of boatbuilding, that unbuilt yacht, the order.

WEGE DURCH DAS LAND

for Katrin Weidemann

Oozy, silent as a jug of milk,
A white snail pours itself into its shell

Near Schwalenberg, in the Westphalian woods
Among goat-bleats, cock-crows and village bells

Where birdsong clears away hot morning traffic,
Letting me clamber back a hundred years

Up muddy trails to when these clustered stones'
Hebrew was carved unaccented by moss,

A sidelined graveyard hummock, silver birches,
Idiomatic testamental names,

Frau Bertha Michaelis, born in the year
Five five eight two, died in five six one nine,

Her calendar dated from the before the Fall –
Caught in a time of cock-crows, village bells,

And light, skittering hooves. Here then, as now,
Snails grew their shells, and on this steep path's loop

Stravaiging peacocks cried, their oriental
Tails undisplayed, with quivering sapphire breasts.

SCOTS AND OFF-SCOTS WORDS

for Brigitte Labs-Ehlert

With the air supremacy of scrambled midges
They land where Air Force One can never land –

<u>Rumgunshoch</u> – broken up with bits of stone –
Savour its tilt, its engine drone, its hold

Loaded with a drop-dead kist of treasures;
<u>Patagium</u> – wing membrane of a bat –

A stealth word, batlike in its loopy swoop,
Out of your ken before you've even twigged;

<u>Jiggirs</u> – insistent pulses: each Scots word's
Frail undercarriage lowers, each sound glides down

On damp runways of grass, in hidden neuks
Where fiddle tunes are hummed in an age of rock,

Words just flown in, turned round without refuelling,
Which, quickly, have already got to go.

PRAYER OF ALLEGIANCE

O God, give me a dangerous pair of hands,
Wee smashers, with the knuckles of John Knox,

Sleekit, though, like Mary Queen of Scots's,
Willow wand wrists – two arm-wrestlers, locked.

Let my five fingers and my other five
Go their own ways, the right ones fanned out, stroking

Uncupped breasts, the other lot skied high
To Javanese stupas. Turn me to a granite sprite,

Head over heels sworn in to each hour's promise,
Day-old patriarch, delicate jack-the-lad,

Nomad who never budged, my alibis
Arthur's Seat, Rotorua, the Black Sea.

ABERDEEN

Port of the re-used Christmas card,
Capital of Doric oil,

Your reputation sluices beyond you,
Shetland's gateway to the south,

Global dorp, helipad of the Shore Porters,
Your undeflectably local paper's

Cobbled headline when the *Titanic* sank,
'Aberdeen Man Drowned.'

Loud on the left side of Scotland's breast,
You are my country's hardened heart,

Macho, Calgachan, missing a beat
Down Union Street, or out on the rigs,

But leaping up, handbagged by laughter
At the Fun Beach's northern lights.

I love your hard core, Marischal College,
Town Hall and tenements, stunner after stunner

Howked out of the Rubislaw Quarry's
Undiamondiferous granite.

THE MUSIC CLEANER

in memory of George Jack

The cleaner pechs at night
Up steep, worn treads of arpeggios,

Polishing, brushing between octaves
With rasping bristles, now and then

Camel hairs for finicky work,
So the song's dust-free again, catches you out.

Relishing the life of Anton Webern
Who stepped outside one night into the curfew,

Lit up a cigarette, and was shot dead,
Songs taken to the cleaners have big souls

Roomy enough for cigarette and gunshot.
Plainchant, birds in spinifex, ululations,

Every song that is must have a cleaner,
To let it know how God is in the details

Public as the sky right now above you,
Private as your own ears, listening.

DREAMERS

Some know they want specific things –
A bergamot, or a Granny Smith –

But others stare so hard at lochans,
They unlearn the usual focus.

Earth-burps, geological yawns
Lure them in to listen hard

To the uvula of the globe,
Where tired commuters to mammoth and elk

Holed up, Delphic aeons before
St Fillan – he of the luminous bones –

Hunkered down at Pittenweem,
Reading by the light of his arm.

JOHN MUIR VARIATIONS

for Les Murray

He hiked a thousand miles to a mountain daisy,
Then travelled, in a great tree, through a storm.

Joe's brush factory's flying metal files
Sliced out his eyesight. Light inched back

Gingerly, a thin, Calvinist boy,
Climbing the castle ruins at Dunbar,

Who'd emigrated from himself, one new
Disciple heading for a Newer World

Among Yosemite's iced, tip-top bird trills,
Riding avalanches with a tyke

Hitched to the universe. Last words:
'Sheep are hoofed locusts. Ban them.' Now he's all

Pastures, moraines, pines, granite, and that odd
Small oil, *Madonna and Child of the Bullfinch*,

At SUNY, Binghamton, where the fat boy, tugging
A string incised on gold, tied to dark claws,

Rewinds yon unhurt bullfinch, flying blind
With zip-code neatness, back to Mary and Jesus

Who's never let go. It homes with a whistlebinkie's
Died-and-gone-to-heaven rush of song.

UIST

South in the north, sun clasped inside the rain,
Levitational birdsong in low fields;

While e-mails graze sand-covered villages
And shaped bone combs comb force-fives in the dunes

I lie down parallel with Grenitote,
Wellies to Udal, head in kidney vetch,

Watching the sly clouds' micromanagement
Of thirty shades of cerulean blue.

June gales have singed the yellow irises,
And frittered silage bags. Behind a croft

Native, cross-bred Hebridean sheep
Scratch themselves on a satellite dish.

Rain's on its way, and so are tides on theirs;
I catch them up, and start to stride across

The machair, thinking of Taigh Chearsabhagh
Where in the sleek museum New Age lettering

Englishes a maybe age-old Gaelic gnomon:
There is no stone but the stream will change its shape.

Croy. Ee. Gaw. Lonker. Pit.
Croy: an animal pen, a rained-on pigsty
Snorting with mooning bums of bacon, snouts
Spikehaired, buxom, Pictish-beasty, rank.
Croy. Ee. Gaw. Lonker. Pit.
Croy. Once, dogging off a dig on the Antonine Wall,
Knees-to-chin in the back of a Beetle near Croy,
I eyed a triumphal arch of Castlecary's
British Empire viaduct above
Turfed-over Roman barracks. Soil had sunk
Castellum, praetorium, and *via*.
Then, *en route* to a *plein air* Latin milestone,
Illegally crossing the motorway,
The car stalled. That coachbuilder with Alexander's Buses,
Spare-time diviner, dowser for lost wells and oak roots,
Revved the engine, stalled the Beetle again
Side-on in front of two great racing lorries.
All five of us, inside our billiard ball,
Unlearned language, trapped in a single breath's
Kyrie eleison, Kyrie eleison
Watching those wall-cabbed artics bearing down
Horns blaring, *AAAAAAAAAAAAAA*,
Doing eighty. Then our engine started.
Ee: an eye, a loophole, a way out,
An opening for water, a delight;
Ee: the eye-opening silent noise of e-mail,
That interruption from another world.
Croy. Ee. Gaw. Lonker. Pit.
Gaw: a Fife word for a drainage furrow.
I walk each day past rows of Pictish graves.
Fife Council's laying mud-brown plastic drainpipes
Down the dead-straight leyline of a Pictish road.
Croy. Ee. Gaw. Lonker. Pit.

Lonker: a hole in a wall, a *yett* through which
Sheep may slip, or a burn, a stream flow under.
Every wall, from Hadrian's to dry-stane-dyke,
Longs for a lonker's
Huddled, nervous rush of living fleece
Against its whinstane, a *vindauga*, a wind's eye, a window
To see through, snow's gurgling, flushing *slàinte!*
Of ice-melt, babbling its lost language,
Baby-talking its way through the WHO GOES THERE?
Croy. Ee. Gaw. Lonker. Pit.
SPEAK ENGLISH! PLAIN ENGLISH! *Naw . . .*
Cry the orphaned *hwll* of *Croy. Ee. Gaw.*
Thrawnly as a couple long and long for a child,
Hopelessly, edgily, until their own stone opens.
Croy. Ee. Gaw. Lonker. Pit.
Pit: to dig holes, marking an edge.
Pit: a portion, or a piece of land, a homestead,
Pittenweem, Pitmillie, Pittodrie, Pittencrieff.
Pit: the only syllable we know
Was born from the obliterated Pictish language –
One landmark cross, perjink on a drowned spire's tip
Whose minster's carved beasts, whorls, and crucifixes
Lie silted, sunk in a Fife-sized, flooded pit.
Croy. Ee. Gaw. Lonker. Pit.
Croy.
Ee.
Gaw.
Lonker.
Pit.

THE MITHRAEUM

God-mulch. Apollo. Coventina.
Snapped-off moons and pre-Christian crosses

Pit the tor. Come-back king,
Midas-touch Mithras, his moorland shrines

Dank caves or knee-high proto-kirks
Northwest of Hexham, waits

First for microbial, then feather-thin,
Then skull-thick, unscabbarded dawn

Butchering the bull-black darkness,
Cutting Christmas Eve's throat.

Mithraic puddles freeze to a golden crunch.
Roads' black ice catches the light.

Hollowed out of the altar's back,
Space for a ceremonial lamp

Set to shine through the holes that petal
Mithras's sun-round head,

From sheep-pee daybreak to sodden gloaming
Keeping the faiths'

Fire lit through ear-burning, toe-nipping cold,
I am the Light of the World.

ARTHUR JOHNSTON

This book contains four translations, or reconventions, of Latin poems by the Aberdeenshire poet Arthur Johnston (1587–1641), who studied at the universities of Aberdeen, Padua, and Sedan. He lived in continental Europe from 1608 until 1632, when he became Lord Rector of King's College, Aberdeen. He died while visiting Oxford. Quirkily classical, Johnston does not pull his punches; 'Glasgow' and 'St Andrews' are from his 'Encomia Urbium', Latin hymns to Scottish towns. As an epigraph to my free, modern versions I quote the words of Dr Winifred Ewing, MSP, in Edinburgh on 12 May 1999: 'The Scottish Parliament, adjourned on 25th March, 1707, is hereby reconvened.'